The "F" Word

by
Don Cermak

Bloomington, IN   Milton Keynes, UK

AuthorHouse™
1663 Liberty Drive, Suite 200
Bloomington, IN 47403
www.authorhouse.com
Phone: 1-800-839-8640

AuthorHouse™ UK Ltd.
500 Avebury Boulevard
Central Milton Keynes, MK9 2BE
www.authorhouse.co.uk
Phone: 08001974150

© *2007 Don Cermak. All rights reserved.*

No part of this book may be reproduced, stored in a retrieval system, or transmitted by any means without the written permission of the author.

First published by AuthorHouse 5/21/2007

ISBN: 978-1-4259-7046-8 (e)
ISBN: 978-1-4259-7045-1 (sc)

Printed in the United States of America
Bloomington, Indiana

This book is printed on acid-free paper.

Library of Congress Control Number: 2006909157

This book is a work of fiction. All of the remarks insinuated under each image are those of the author and in no way meant to critique, alter or change the meaning of the classic films used, nor are they intended to denigrate any historical events or disparage the character or reputation of any person living or dead.

While many of the author's own photographs and paintings have been used in the compilation of this booklet, grateful acknowledgement and thanks is given for permission to Xerox photographs from the following copyrighted material:

Time, Inc Time Annual 2005 Special Collector's Edition, The Year in Review.
Copyright @ 2005 Time, Inc. Home Entertainment
LIFE: Our Century In Pictures A Bullfinch Press Book
Little, Brown and Company Copyright © 1999 by Time.
People Celebrates the 70's
Copyright © 2000 Time, Inc. Home Entertainment.
100 Greatest TV Stars of Our Time
Copyright © 2003 Time, Inc. Published by People Books.

RENOIR: Bather Pushing up her hair. Detroit Institute of Art
 Copyright © 1987 Hugh Lauter Levin Associates, Inc.
 © 1985 by Editions d'Art Albert Skira S.A. Geneva
 published in U.S. in 1985 by Rizzoli International Publications, Inc
PICASSO: Cabeza, 1972-Lucerna, Galerie Rosengart
Portrait of Gertrude Stein, Metropolitan Museum of Art
REMBRANDT: The Jewish Bride - Rijksmuseum, Amsterdam
Photofest, Inc.
Cobal Collection
Library of Congress
National Archives

Henry Ford Museum
Eastman Kodak Co
Janzten, Inc
Clipper Magazine © 2006
Christian Science Monitor

To Lois

For putting up with my
    craziness and profanity
In rehearsing my selections
    for inclusion in this book
Until she finally had to tell me
To shut the &%$# up

INTRODUCTION

When I received an email listing the six places in time where the "F" word could be used, indicated on the back cover, I also felt the "F" word was one of the better ways to accurately comment on the event at hand. I enjoyed the humor and made copies to pass out to a number of my friends.

One of the comments that most frequently got back to me was, "I'll bet there are other instances in time where the "F" word could have been used."

In my research I discovered a plethora of other occasions in history, as well as in current events, that qualified for such an expletive to properly comment on the event, and accompanied them with appropriate photographs or drawings for your enjoyment.

The dictionary defines the word expletive as 1. an oath or exclamation 2. a word, phrase, etc. not needed for the sense but used merely to fill out a sentence or metrical line, for grammar, rhythm, balance, etc. 3. anything serving as a filler - adj. Used to fill out a sentence, line, etc.

When one thinks about this, the "F" word can be considered one of the most frequently used words ever created whose etymology is not found in any dictionary.

It's F--- this, or F--- that, or F--- you, or the F--- you say, or he's a F---ing jerk, or shut the F--- up, or F---off, and the ever popular you're F---ing A well right.

When a person is involved in a stressful situation you can double its use in spades. It can be a noun, a verb, adverb, subject, predicate - whatever - whose salient use has made it recognizable by everyone. It is unconscionably used by men, women and even children every day out of context so as to create its own *genre* of usage. I've even heard some people say they believe it is a vernacular created by African Americans because of its frequency of use in their conversations.

The absence from dictionaries of old, well-known vulgate terms for sexual and excretory organs and functions is not due to lack of citations for these words but suggest, rather, that they are so well known as to require no explanation.

If a Professor at Princeton University could write the book 'On Bull Shit', I asked myself why couldn't I write about the word most associated to procreation (fornication) that is most commonly replaced by the "F" word used by everyone. That's how this book came to be.

I discovered that the Pilgrims were most probably responsible for the popularity of the "F" word because of their unusual type of punishment for crimes. When a person was found guilty of adultery they were punished by being put on public display in a stockade with a sign hanging from their neck that read 'For Unlawful Carnal Knowledge.' The Acronym, formed from this saying became the popular name calling game of the day, no matter what the offense. This fad caught on and carried right on through to modern times.

Symbolic logic in mathematics uses special symbols for propositions quantifiers, and relationships among propositions. The symbols I have chosen to represent the "F" word are &%$# and &%$#!@* for the present participle, as in fighting.

As you read this booklet, I'm sure you will be able to come up with more than a few occasions of your own where the "F" word fits right in to characterize some person, thing or event in your life. Think about the consternation of the person in the instances presented that prompted their use of the "F" word. Put yourself in that person's shoes and try to think of something better to say to vent your anger. It's hard to top the "F" word, isn't it?

Okay, now repeat one of the occasions in this book to your friends using the "F" word itself for shock value. It should evoke a snicker or guffaw or both. If you get no reaction - just a blank stare - or they make a dour face, these so-called friends really don't know you. Either that or they don't know much about the history of this country, aren't up on current events, have a poor sense of humor or haven't been to a movie lately, are prudes, or worse yet, are pedantic and should be relegated from your *Alpha* list of friends to your *Omega* list if not dropped altogether.

Let me add, that when I was younger, I always found it difficult to use the "F" word. I felt the use of such a word was a sign of weakness or ignorance at not being able to express myself more accurately. To this day I still prefer to use other exclamations or descriptive adjectives in conversation. I must admit, however, there are times when no other word gives me the personal satisfaction, or closure to an argument than the "F" word does.

I'm not advocating you start using the "F" word indiscriminately. I'm just saying it can be a good argument-closer, unless of course, you come up against experts in the art of disseminating this expletive like the Tony Soprano family and associates.

I hope this booklet brings a little laughter into your life and lets you release any pent up energy you might have stored away, because laughter really is therapeutic and will do you a &%$#!@* lot of good in coping with what is happening in the world today.

The "F" Word /11

"YOU TOLD ME YOU HAD A &%$#!@ VASECTOMY!"
Angelina Jolie to Brad Pitt 2006

"NO, MY HAND ISN'T COLD. I JUST GOT A &%$#!@* ITCH I CAN'T GET TO."
Napoleon, 1780

Louvre Book Shop, Paris

"No, that isn't my mother. I don't even know who the &%$# my mother is."
Leonardo da Vinci

"It's Christmas, it's freezing out, I'm pregnant - God only knows how - and now you tell me you forgot to book a &%$#!@* room at the Inn! Terrific!"
Mary to Joseph

The "F" Word /13

I don't know about you, honey, but if that horny Leo comes around, I've got a &%$#!@* headache."
A pair of Lionesses on the sun-dried Savanna

"Watch where you put that soap, shorty, or you're &%$#!@* dead."
Clint Eastwood, High Plains Drifter, 1973

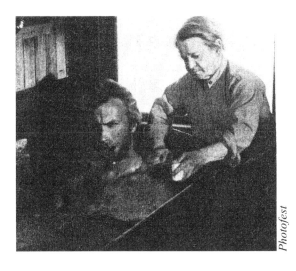

The "F" Word /14

"WHAT THE &%$# DO YOU MEAN I SWEAR TOO &%$#!@* MUCH, &%$#FACE? I SHOULD PUNCH YOUR &%$#!@* LIGHTS OUT FOR MAKING THAT RAW &%$#!@* REMARK."

Jack Nicholson, The Shining, 1980

"WHO WAS THE &%$#!@* LOOKOUT THAT YELLED, "LOOK AT THE TITS. DROP ANCHOR?"

Christopher Columbus 1492

What about this Conundrum?

Abraham Lincoln was elected to Congress in 1846
John F Kennedy was elected to Congress in 1946
Lincoln was elected President in 1860
Kennedy was elected President in 1960
Both were particularly concerned with civil rights
Both wives lost children while living in the White House
Both men were shot on a Friday
Both men were shot in the head
Now it really gets &%$#!@* weird
Lincoln's secretary was named Kennedy
Kennedy's secretary was named Lincoln
Both were assassinated by southerners
Both were succeeded by Southerners named Johnson
Andrew Johnson who succeeded Lincoln was born in 1808
Lyndon Johnson who succeeded Kennedy was born in 1908
John Wilkes Booth was born in 1839
Lee Harvey Oswald was born in 1939
Both assassins were known by their three names
Both names are composed of fifteen letters
Now hang onto your &%$#!@* seats
Lincoln was shot at a theatre named 'Ford'
Kennedy was shot in a car called 'Lincoln' made by 'Ford'
Lincoln was shot in a theatre and his assassin
ran and hid in a warehouse
Kennedy was shot from a warehouse and his
assassin ran and hid in a theatre
Booth and Oswald were both assassinated before their trial

And here's the &%$#!@* kicker
A week before Lincoln was shot he was in Monroe, Maryland
A week before Kennedy was shot he was in Marilyn Monroe

Is this &%$#!@* creepy or what?
Have a history teacher explain it to you if they can

The "F" Word /16

Copyist Don Cermak, 1994

Eyes That Talk

"Photographed by Steve McCurry in 1984, this 16 yr. old Afgan refugee made the cover of National Geographic in 1985 It was her green eyes flecked with yellow and blue that fascinated me more than her haunting look. With me it's always the eyes when I paint. To capture a person I must get the eyes right. So I kept the picture and put it in a book but completely forgot which &%$#!@* book it was. It wasn't until we were unpacking, after moving to Florida, that I found it again and copied it in pastels. It has been hanging on our dinning room wall next to Anthony Quinn's 'Zorba, Self Portrait' (page 87) since 1994.

It was a nice quiet day in New Orleans before Katrina hit and than all hell broke loose and everything did get &%$#!@* crazy at Shirley's place.

Don Cermak, 1994

"Fidel Castro is a &%$#!@* young, 26 yr old upstart who won't last a year in power."
President Batista ousted in the 1959 Cuban revolution

"When I won my sixth they started calling it the &%$#!@* Tour de Lance."
Lance Armstrong after winning the Tour de France in 2004

The "F" Word /18

"I KNOW WHAT THE &%$# I LIKE TO DO TO RAVEL'S 'BOLERO' HOW ABOUT YOU?"
Bo Derek in Ten, 1979

"I DON'T KNOW WHY THEY EJECTED ME. SO I BUTTED HIM. SO WHAT? IT'S ALL A PART OF THE &%$#!@* GAME."
French soccer star Zinedine Zidane, World Cup 2006
(Sticks and stones may break bones, but words can break your focus)

"SOME DUMB &%$# ALWAYS YELLS, "NOTHIN' BUT NET" OR "YOU DA MAN" AT SPORTING EVENTS."
Michael Jordan

THERE ARE TWO KINDS OF PEDESTRIANS: THE &%$#!@* QUICK AND THE &%$#!@* DEAD.
(A ponderism)

The "F" Word / 19

Rembrandt: Rijksmuseum, Amsterdam

"Don't worry. My dear, I know the
&%$#!@* Heim-Lich maneuver!"
Rembrandt's The Jewish Bride, 1668

"You say you want to know how Michelle Wie hits those &%$#!@* 300-yard drives? With her driver, you dumb dipshit, that's how."

"Okay, whose the &%$#!@* idiot that put that bar of soap on my balance beam?"
Nadia Comanici, 1976 Olympics

"The owners of this colorful restaurant located at 10 Sukhumvit Soi 12 in Bangkok are proponents of planned parenthood and practice what they preach. When you pay your bill, instead of receiving mints, you can have all the &%$#!@* condoms you want."

The Cermaks dined there and enjoyed the fine Thai Cuisine

"The blues? I just puts my &%$#!@* lips together and blows. Das all."

Louis Armstrong

The "F" Word /22

"WHAT THE &%$# ARE YOU LOOKING AT?"
Lady Godiva

"AND JUST WHERE DO YOU SUGGEST WE KEEP
ALL THIS &%$#!@* GOLD?"
Director of Fort Knox to Director of the Mint

"EVERYONE'S WATCHING NOW SO IF YOU'LL JUST
STAND STILL FOR A SECOND WE CAN GET INTO THE
SWING OF THINGS AND GET THIS &%$#!@* THING
OVER WITH."
Ling Ling to Sling Sling, Gift pandas from China
after President Nixon's visit in 1972

The "F" Word /23

"I MAY LOOK LIKE A &%$#!@* BUM, BUT YOU
SHOULD NEVER JUDGE A BOOK BY ITS COVER.
READ MY BOOKS FIRST, THEN JUDGE ME."

Leo Tolstoy -
Anna Karenina
War & Peace

The "F" Word /24

Charles Fischer Collection — Copyist Don Cermak 2005

IN 2005, PICASSO'S 'BOY WITH A PIPE' BECAME THE WORLD'S MOST EXPENSIVE &%$#!@* PIECE OF ART WHEN IT SOLD AT AUCTION AT SOTHEBY'S FOR A RECORD $104.2 MILLION.

Pablo Picasso, 1905
Formerly in the collection of Mr & Mrs John Hay Whitney

IF YOU LEND SOMEONE MONEY AND NEVER SEE THAT PERSON AGAIN, IT WAS PROBABLY &%$#!@* WORTH IT.

NEVER TAKE LIFE TOO &%$#!@* SERIOUSLY. NOBODY GETS OUT ALIVE ANYWAY.

(A Ponderism)

August Rodin 1840-1917
"We saw his Thinker in Paris outside the Rodin Museum - an ancient 18th century mansion (formerly the Hotel Biron) - which is just around the corner from Napoleon's Tomb at the Invalides."

The Author

"I CAN'T &%$#!@* THINK OF WHAT IT WAS THAT I WAS TRYING TO REMEMBER, NOW!"
Rodin's Thinker

FIRST I FAKED CHASTITY. THEN I FAKED ORGASMS. NOW I FAKE &%$#!@* FIDELITY.

Girlie talk

"Well if it isn't my old &%$#!@* zoo keeper. Come'er and gimme a hug, kid."

Copyist Don Cermak 2007

"I ONLY WANTED SOME DUMB &%$# TO LOVE ME FOR MY BRAINS AND I GOT LUCKY AND GOT ARTHUR MILLER. AIN'T LOVE BLIND?"

Mansell © Time, Inc

"YOU TELL ANYONE I LIKE TO WEAR SILK PANTIES AND I'LL &%$#!@* BLOW YOU AWAY."

J. Edgar Hoover, FBI Director

AP / Wide World

"WHAT DO YOU MEAN, I SHOULD &%$#!@* GROW UP?"

Wilt Chamberlin - scored 100 pts vs. N.Y. Knicks, in 1962

The "F" Word /28

"SEE WHAT HAPPENS WHEN YOU STICK YOUR
&%$#!@* FINGER IN A WALL SOCKET?"

Lon Chaney,
Phantom of the Opera, 1928

IT SAYS IT'S AN ATTEMPT TO CREATE ORDER WHILE
SIMULTANEOUSLY EMBRACING FREEDOM, ULTIMATELY
ESTABLISHING UNITY THROUGH THE HARMONIOUS
INTERACTION OF SEEMINGLY INCONGRUOUS ELEMENTS.

The "F" Word / 29

"Why the &%$# do they allow people to bring guns into a police station?"
Lee Harvey Oswald, 1963

"Someone told me to go fly a kite. So I did and you won't believe what the &%$# happened?"
Benjamin Franklin, 1751

The "F" Word /30

"LITTLE &%$#!@* FISH MY ASS. WE'RE
GONNA NEED A BIGGER BOAT."
Sheriff Roy Scheider in Jaws, 1975

"HOW MANY TIMES DO I HAVE TO TELL YOU
THE SONG GOES, "I'VE GOT A LOVELY BUNCH OF
COCONUTS," NOT A &%$#!@* BUNCH...?"

HAVE YOU NOTICED SINCE EVERYONE HAS A
&%$#!@* CAMCORDER THESE DAYS NO ONE
TALKS ABOUT UFO'S LIKE THEY USE TO!

(A Ponderism)

The "F" Word /31

"Yo dawg, you ain't gonna believe what the &%$# Simon just said to Paula!"
American Idol Judge, Randy Jackson

"Now I know what the &%$# they mean when they say this is the I.C.U. floor!"

The "F" Word /32

Rembrandt Self Portrait- Copyist Don Cermak 1993

Rembrandt 1606-69
Master of the Dutch Golden Age of Painters

"Looking for a Rembrandt?"

This close up of Rembrandt's head, by copyist Don Cermak, is from a full body portrait by the artist. "The year 2006 marks the 400th birthday of Rembrandt Harmensz van Rijn. At one point there were 670 paintings attributed to him, but since the Rembrandt Research Project compiled a definitive catalogue, downgrading works done by pupils and imitators and worse, this number has been cut in half. Currently, there are only about fourteen in the world still privately owned which can be had for under $50 &%$#!@* million. So better hurry up or you'll miss out on these bargains!"

The Author

Copyist Don Cermak 1994

"I was in Athens, Greece in 1994 when Burt Lancaster died of a heart attack the month before his 81st birthday. It made me think about the time he waved and gave me that great smile of his. He had purchased a home in Florida after filming 'Birdman of Alcatraz'. I saw him in his front yard as I was driving by and honked. He waved and flashed that smile.

"I read that he had suffered a stroke in 1990 that left him partially paralysed and thought how &%$#!@* devastating that must have been for this man who was a one-time circus acrobat and a great athlete. I can still picture that smile."

The Author

WHEN EVERYTHING'S COMING YOUR WAY, YOU'RE PROBABLY IN THE WRONG &%$#!@* LANE.

> "C'MON, ABDULLA, IT'S ONLY A FEW &%$#!@* MILES, JUST A GOOD STRETCH OF THE LEGS."
>
> The Author on his first camel ride in Cairo

> "YOU CAN TALK TO A FADE, BUT A &%$#!@* HOOK WON'T LISTEN."
>
> Lee Trevino

> "I WANT TO THANK THE NAACP FOR GIVING ME THIS &%$#!@* TROPHY."
>
> Dean Martin cradling Sammy Davis Jr. in his Arms at a meeting of the "Rat Pack' in Las Vegas

"I GUESS YOU WEREN'T SO &%$#!@* LUCKY AFTER ALL, WERE YA PUNK?"
Clint Eastwood, Dirty Harry

"YOU CAN TAKE THAT &%$#!@* DOBEDOBEDO OUT OF HERE AND SHOVE IT 'CAUSE IT'LL NEVER SELL."
Frank Sinatra in Pal Joey, 1957

THE ONLY DIFFERENCE BETWEEN A &%$#!@*
RUT AND A GRAVE IS THE DEPTH.

(A Ponderism)

"DID YOU MAKE ALL THAT &%$#!@* BROWN STUFF IN
THOSE PRETTY WHITE BUBBLES FOR MOMMY, HONEY?"

"HOW MANY &%$#!@* GIRLS DID YOU
SAY MY WIFE GAVE BIRTH TO?"

Annette, Cecille, Emilie, Marie & Yvonne
make five by my count, Mr. Dionne

"WHO STARTED THE &%$#!@* RUMOR THAT
I DROPPED AN APPLE FROM A TREE?"

Isaac Newton, 1670

IN THE 60'S PEOPLE TOOK ACID TO MAKE THE
WORLD WEIRD. NOW THE WORLD IS WEIRD AND
PEOPLE TAKE PROZAC TO MAKE IT NORMAL.

(A Ponderism)

"I KNOW I CAN MAKE IT IF I CAN JUST KEEP MY
&%$#!@* FEET FROM FALLING ASLEEP 'CAUSE
WHEN THAT HAPPENS I GOTTA STAND UP."

Charles Lindberg - N.Y. to Paris, 1927

"BEING THE FIRST MAN ON THE MOON WASN'T
THE ONLY THING FOR ME IN 1969, IT WAS HITTING
THAT &%$#!@* GOLF BALL OVER 400 YARDS THAT
WAS COOL. EAT YOUR HEART OUT, TIGER."

Neil Armstrong

"A GOOD LAWYER KNOWS THE LAW, BUT A GREAT
LAWYER KNOWS THE &%$#!@* JUDGE."

Al Capone

"IF YOU THINK IT'S HARD TO MEET NEW PEOPLE, TRY
PICKING UP THE WRONG &%$#!@* GOLF BALL."

Jack Lemmon

The "F" Word /38

"I'M ORIGINALLY FROM OHIO AND THIS POLITICAL CARTOON APPEARED IN OUR PAPER - THE CLEVELAND PLAIN DEALER FEB 12, 1984. DOES THIS QUALIFY AS A &%$#!@* DEJA-VU?"
The Author

The "F" Word / 39

"WE'RE GONNA CRAP THUNDER AND SPIT LIGHTNING WHEN WE GET TOGETHER, BABY, 'CAUSE YOU'RE MY &%$#!@* KIND OF WOMAN."
Boris Karloff to Elsa Lancaster in Bride of Frankenstein, 1935

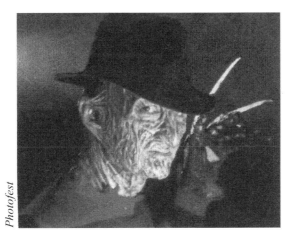

"YOU THINK YOUR PSORIASIS IS BAD? I DON'T KNOW WHAT THE &%$# I GOT."
Robert Englund, A Nightmare on Elm Street, 1984

The "F" Word /40

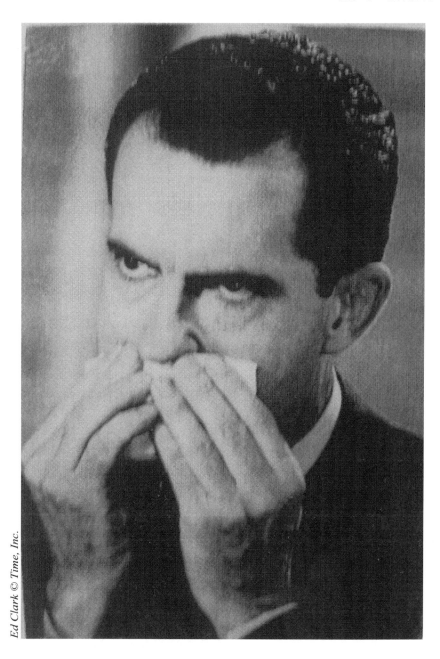

"TAPE? I NEVER RECORDED ANYTHING IN MY LIFE." OH WHAT A &%$#!@* TANGLED WEB WE WEAVE, WHEN FIRST WE PRACTICE TO DECEIVE.

Richard Nixon & Watergate

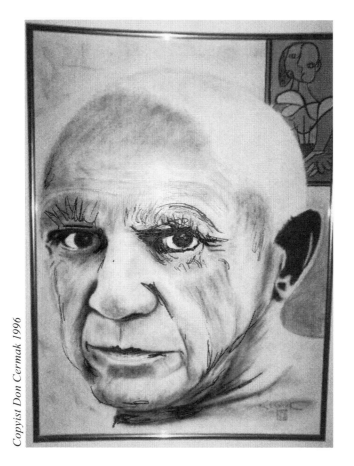

Copyist Don Cermak 1996

Here's an image of the anarchist himself who started every &%$#!@* thing: Impressionism, Cubism, Surrealism, Classical and Abstracts, smashing precedents, defying convention and transforming reality every time he picked up a brush. He found the astonishing in the ordinary and made everything he drew exciting. He was ironic, tragic, comic, bitter, but always fascinating. He said, "For me, art has neither past nor future. All I have ever made was made for the present."
Pablo Picaso 1881-1973
(This is the Author's portrait of Picasso after he visited the Picasso Museum in Madrid in 1996)

Cermak Collection, 1987

"We met Mr. Quinn in 1987 at his Premiere Exhibition at the Center Art Galleries-Hawaii where he stunned the art world with his "La Femme Ideal" - a stirring tribute he dedicated to all of his ideal women. with the debut of his painting and sculpture, he was proclaimed the fine art discovery of the decade. I was very impressed with his work and didn't have enough &%$#!@* money to buy an original but I did manage this hand-signed, limited-edition (No 63 of 100) self-portrait serigraph, which is hung on our dinning room wall between Vermeer's 'Girl With a Pearl Earring' (Page 68) and the girl from Afghanistan (page 16)"

The Author

"Ollie always said I could have been a &%$#!@* brain surgeon if only I put my mind to it."

Stan Laurel, the comic genius behind Laurel and Hardy Fame

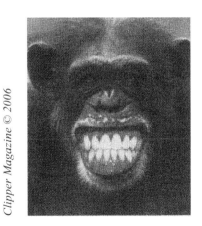

You don't have to floss all your &%$#!@* teeth...

Just the ones you want to keep!

"I KNOW YOU LOVE DIAMONDS, HONEY, BUT YOU BETTER BE CAREFUL 'CAUSE YOUR OWN &%$#!@* GEMS ARE STARTING TO BUST LOOSE."
Richard Burton to Liz Taylor

"I DON'T KNOW WHETHER OR NOT THIS &%$#!@* NOVELTY WILL CATCH ON."
George Eastman, 1988

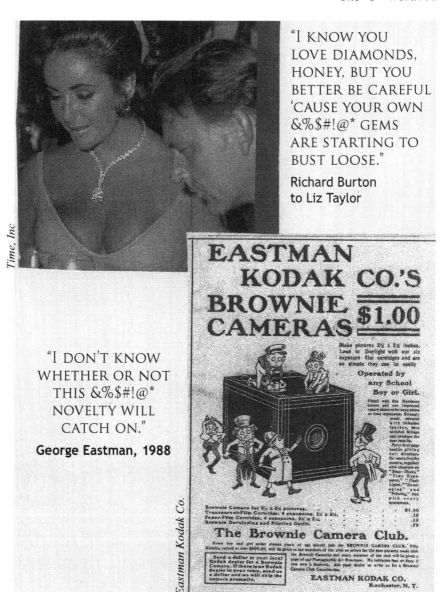

"IF I'M PLAYING GOLF AND I SEE LIGHTENING, I GET INSIDE &%$#!@* FAST. IF GOD WANTS TO PLAY THROUGH, LET HIM."
Bob Hope

So you think you know everything?
Did you know...

- A cat has 32 muscles in each ear
- A crocodile cannot stick out its tongue
- Coca Cola was originally green
- A shark is the only fish that can blink with both eyes
- All 50 states are listed across the top of the Lincoln Memorial on the back of the $5 bill
- Almonds are a member of the peach family
- An ostrich's eye is bigger than its brain
- Butterflies taste with their feet
- Babies are born without kneecaps. They don't appear until ages 2-6
- Dreamt is the only English word that ends in the letters "mt".
- No word in the English language rhymes with month, orange, silver, or purple.
- Peanuts are one of the ingredients of dynamite.
- There are 293 ways to make change for a dollar.
- Tigers have striped skin, not just striped fur
- Your stomach has to produce a new layer of mucus every two weeks otherwise it will digest itself
- If the population of China walked past you, in single file, the line would never end because of their rate of reproduction.
- The cruise liner QE2 moves only six inches per gallon of fuel
- The Winter of 1932 was so cold Niagara Falls froze completely solid
- Our eyes are always the same size from birth, but our ears and nose never stop growing
- The words "Racecar", "Kayak", and "Level" are palindromes - they Read and are spelled the same forward and backwards Do you know what the longest Palindrome is?
- Only four words end in "dous" Tremendous, Horrendous, Stupendous. Can you name the last one?
- Only two words contain all five vowels IN ORDER. Name them.

Now you know almost every &%$#!@* thing.

To complete your education turn to page 106

Copyist Don Cermak 1993

"Don't compare me to Picasso. I'm my own &%$#!@* man."
A Glance in the Mirror by Anthony Quinn, 1985

All of us could take a lesson from the &%$#!@* weather. It pays no attention to critics.
(A ponderism)

The easiest way to find something lost around the House is to buy a &%$#!@* replacement.
(A Ponderism)

The "F" Word /47

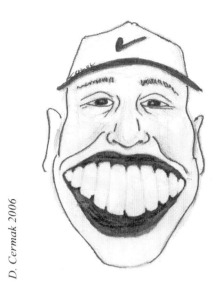

"YOU DON'T THINK I CAN GET THIS ON THE &%$#!@* GREEN FROM HERE. JUST WATCH ME."
Tiger Woods to a heckler

"YOU STARTED AT THE AGE OF 5 AND COMPOSED HOW MANY &%$#!@* CONCERTOS?"
Wolfgang Amadeous Mozart, 1756

"DON'T TELL ME HOW TO WRAP. I'VE BEEN
&%$#!@* WRAPPING ALL OVER THE WORLD."
Christo

The artist who calls his projects "Irrational and absolutely unnecessary" and his wife. Jeanne-Claude, were instrumental in getting the Gates Project for Central Park in New York approved which, on Feb. 12, 2005 hung 1,092,200 square feet of saffron-colored panels of mylon cloth, each 8 1/2 feet long, from 7,500 16 foot-high steel frames, along 27 miles of park walkways, at a cost of 21 million. They have been doing things like this all over the world for the past four decades.

"WE BELONG TO THE FBI* YOU WANT TO JOIN
OUR &%$#!@* CLUB. IT'S CALLED THE MOTHERS
AND FATHERS ITALIAN ASSOCIATION.
Liotta, DeNiro, Sorvino, Peschi - Goodfellas, 1990
*FBI - Full Blooded Italians

The "F" Word /49

"I'M JUST GOING TO TAKE IT OUT FOR A LITTLE SPIN. WHAT THE &%$# COULD HAPPEN?"
James Dean, 1955

"WHO I &%$# AND WHEN I &%$# IS NO &%$#!@* BUSINESS OF YOURS."
Jeff Bridges to brother Beau in The Fabulous Baker Boys

The "F" Word /50

"Who say Ima smell fromma too mucha &%$#ink garleek?"
Mussolini

"So, Roger, how does it feel to beat the world record holder, John Landy?"

"My &%$#!@* legs are killing me."

Roger Bannister
August 16, 1954 3.58.8

"How much? Hey, man, I just want a &%$#!@* cup of coffee. I don't want to buy the store!"
First time customer at Starbucks

Starbucks brochure

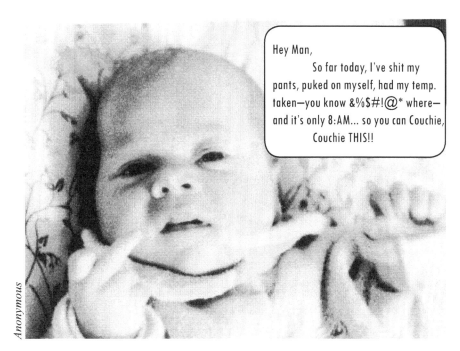
Anonymous

Hey Man,
So far today, I've shit my pants, puked on myself, had my temp. taken—you know &%$#!@* where— and it's only 8:AM... so you can Couchie, Couchie THIS!!

"Golf and sex are about the only &%$#!@* things you can enjoy withouth being good at."
Jimmey Demaret

The "F" Word /52

D. Cermak 2006

"WHAT DO YOU MEAN I HAVE TO GET UP AT
&%$#!@* 2 AM TO FEED THE BABY OR I'M FIRED?"
Donald Trump

Mayong River, Bali

"EVERYONE WHO WANTS TO GO OVER THE
&%$#!@* FALLS RAISE THEIR OARS."

Okay, Houdini, you had your fun now where's my &%$#!@* bra?"

The "F" Word /55

"YOU WEREN'T &%$#!@* KIDDING WHEN YOU SAID THE SQUARE REALLY FLOODS WHEN THE TIDE COMES IN."
First time visitor to Piazza San Marco

"Golf is a game in which you yell "fore", shoot six, and write down a &%$#!@* five."
Paul Harvey

"I never said I was a &%$#!@* angel, did I?"
O.J. Simpson

"I hear Booths' pretty &%$#!@* good. Make reservations for his first performance for me."
Abraham Lincoln at Ford's Theater, 1865

"You want a bite of my &%$#!@* apple, Adam?"
Barbara Stanwyck The Lady Eve 1941

Picasso's Madam X, 1954 – Copyist Don Cermak

"PICASSO MADE HIS 4ᵀᴴ WIFE (JACQUELINE ROGUE) PUT ON A TURKISH COSTUME SO HE COULD PAINT HER.

The story goes that she surprised him one day by making some sweet Turkish Halvah (his favorite dessert). It so delighted him that he spontaneously asked her to pose for him, Something he had never done before - although he had made dozens of sketches of her from memory. He made her put on a Turkish costume and began what he called 'destroying his sketch' using her face, limbs, and torso as unrelated objects. He drew her in the classical manner, then as a succession of cubes, then in boldly simplified outlines – on and on – one variation after another incorporating different styles as he went on. Jacqueline later said it was like watching a &%$#!@* magician at work.

After she went to sleep, he stayed up most of the night working on the painting which remained in his private collection until he allowed it to be photographed years later. This is the author's rendition of that oil painting in pastels.

The "F" Word /58

D. Cermak Nairobi Safari 1986

"Hey Noah! You were supposed to bring on two of each &%$#!@* species, but a few of us still haven't seen our significant other yet. Let's be for gettin on the by God ball."

The "F" Word /59

"Hey Mo! Hey Larry! A gal here says she's a &%$#!@* hooker and I'm no golfer so what do I do to straighten her out? N'yuk! N'yuk! N'yuk! N'yuk!"
Curly Howard of The Three Stooges

"What the &%$# was it, one if by land or two?"
Paul Revere, 1775

"Frankly, Scarlet, I don't give a damn. There, I said it and I'm &%$#!@* glad."
Clark Gable - Gone With The Wind, 1939

"What the &%$# do we care if
second place pays a lot!"
Michelson, Els, Singh, Garcia, Furyk etal PGA members.

"Its' a little invention that I've been working
on that I call a Horseless buggy. It may
not be &%$#!@* much, but I'm trying."
Henry Ford 1900-1923

"I would like to deny all allegations by Bob
Hope that during my last game of golf,
I hit an eagle and a &%$#!@* moose."
Gerald Ford

The "F" Word /61

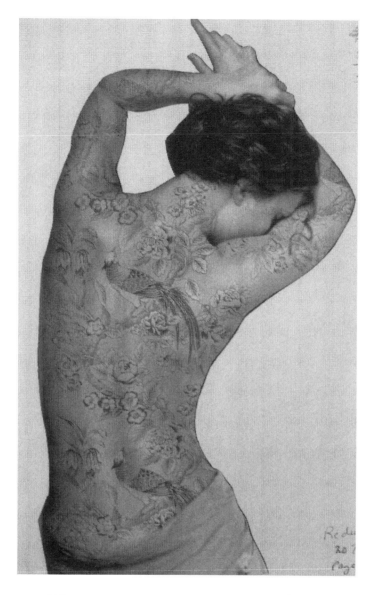

We told you not to get a &%$#!@* tattoo when you've been drinking.

"Pro golfers make a lot of &%$#!@* money. Both my ex-wives are so rich that neither of their husbands work."
Lee Trevino

D. Cermak Nairobi Safari 1986

"Don't ask! I don't know whether they're &%$#!@* black with white stripes or white with black stripes."

Zoo Keeper

Copyist Don Cermak 2007

"Whadaya mean it looks like I just spilled &%$#!@* paint all over the floor? I'm an Abstract Expressionist, and don't call me Jack the Dripper."

Jackson Pollock won U.S. Postal Service endorsement but they took artistic license in basing its stamp on a Martha Holmes photo; it painted out Pollock's ever-present cigarette.

"I WONDER WHAT WILBER AND ORVILLE WOULD SAY TODAY IF THEY KNEW MY PLANE FLEW AROUND THE WORLD ON ONLY ONE &%$#!@* TANK OF GAS IN 1986?"

Burt Rutan's propeller driven aircraft - Voyager

WHEN JUDY GARLAND WAS 16 SHE HAD TO HAVE HER BREASTS PAINFULLY TAPED FLAT EVERY DAY TO PLAY THE 12-YEAR OLD DOROTHY.

"I DON'T THINK WE'RE IN &%$#!@* KANSAS ANY MORE, TOTO."

Judy Garland, The Wizard of OZ

"I CAN GET YOU BETTY GRABLE, BUT WHAT THE
&%$# DO YOU WANT A HAMMER FOR IN HERE?"
Morgan Freeman to Tim Robbins
Shawshank Redemption, 1994

"I MUST FIND A WC BECAUSE I HAVE BEEN DRINKING
A &%$#!@* LOT SINCE MY HUNGER STRIKE."
Mahatma Gandhi 1869-1918
India's Apostle of Non-Violence

The "F" Word /65

Copyist Don Cermak 1995

"IF YOU WOULD ONLY STOP STEPPING ON MY &%$#!@*
TOES I THINK WE COULD FINALLY FINISH THIS DANCE."
Renoir's Dancing at Bougival, 1883

"WHO THE &%$# SAID I WAS TONE DEAF?"
Wolfgang Amadeous Mozart, 1781

"COMPETITIVE GOLF IS PLAYED ON A &%$#!@* 5
INCH COURSE: THE SPACE BETWEEN YOUR EARS."
Bobby Jones

The "F" Word /66

"WHY DIDN'T YOU GET CLOSER TO SHORE? MY
&%$#!@* SHOES ARE GETTING SOAKED."
General Douglas MacArthur - Manila 1951

"IF THAT BALL WAS WRAPPED IN BACON EVEN
LASSIE COULDN'T FIND IT. WE CALL THAT
A AMF - AUDIOS MOTHER&%$#ER.
A John Daly drive

"THE MAFIA IS NOT ABOUT THE MOB. IT'S ABOUT THE
VICISSITUDES OF THE ITALIAN-AMERICAN FAMILY LIFE
AND THE PERILS OF MAINTAINING TRADITION IN
THE &%$#!@* FACE OF ASSIMILATION: A METAPHOR
FOR THE AMERICAN IMMIGRATION EXPERIENCE."
Allen Barra, The Baltimore Sun 2006

The "F" Word /67

I SAID ONE BOTTLE, NOT ONE &%$#!@* CUP, IF YOU WANT TO MASTER THE ART OF FRENCH COOKING."
Julia Child, 1916-2004

"WHAT THE &%$# DID YOU SAY SHE WAS DOING IN BED, FATHER?"
Question to the priest in the Exorcist, 1973

Vermeer 1665/66 – Copyist Don Cermak 1996

The Girl With a Pearl Earring
Johannes Vermeer 1632-1675

"This is considered the Dutch Mona Lisa. It was on display at the National Gallery in Washington, DC where I saw it in 1996 before it was returned to the Mauritshius Gallery in The Hague, Netherlands. When you stand up close and look into her hazel-grey eyes they shine with lifelike transparency, and there is something that is actually compelling about her. Her eyes are wide open yet she remains as opaque as the black background behind her. I bought a &%$#!@* poster and did a pastel because I fell for that indefinable quality we call art."

The Author

SUDOCU FOR &%$#!@* DUMMIES

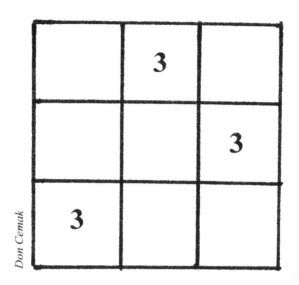

THE APPLE PIE CAMPAIGN

Ben & Jerry sold out to the Dutch conglomerate Unilever in the yr. 2,000 but are now disillusioned that they have not pursued the vision of social responsibility they were involved in. They want to change our country's spending priorities. Instead of maintaining 10,000 nuclear bombs they are advocating spending that money for kid's programs. If it ever comes down to a war how &%$#!@* many are we going to need? 5? 10? Certainly not 10,000 bombs!

So they are coming out with a new American Pie flavor ice cream that will carry information on the carton lids about how to get involved in this with them.

The "F" Word /70

"Hah! So now you zee vhat happens vhen ve split dat &%$#!@* atom!"
Albert Einstein, 1944

She coined the phrase "The Lost Generation" for the struggling, but stylish young writers of the day – Hemmingway Sherwood Anderson etal

"If you think Picasso's portrait of me looks bad, you should see some of his other &%$#!@* stuff."
Gertrude Stein

The "F" Word /71

Lucerne, Gallerie, Rosenguart

"Who the &%$# is that supposed
to be, Pablo, yo momma?"
Picasso's 'Cabeza', 1972

"You want me to take two of each &%$#!@* what?"
Noah 4314 BC

"Tell the &%$#!@* Swiss guards we won't
be needing them today. We'll just be
riding around St. Peter's Square."
Head bodyguard for Pope John Paul II the day he was shot, 1981

The "F" Word /72

"WE HATED THE &%$#!@* COLORS ANYWAY."
Comment from people tearing down the Berlin wall

"HOW MANY TIMES DO I HAVE TO TELL YOU, MY NAME HAS A &%$#!@* "O", NOT AN "A".
Claude Monet

HEALTH IS MERELY THE SLOWEST &%$#!@* POSSIBLE RATE AT WHICH ONE CAN DIE!
(A Ponderism)

"DON'T TRY TO B.S. ME. I KNOW WHAT THE &%$# YOU WERE DOING IN THE OVAL OFFICE."
Hillary Rodham Clinton, 1999

"IT TOOK ME 17 YEARS TO GET 3,000 HITS IN BASEBALL. I DID IT IN ONE &%$#!@* AFTERNOON ON THE GOLF COURSE."
Hank Aaron

The "F" Word /73

FALLINGWATER
THE MOST FAMOUS PRIVATE RESIDENCE EVER BUILT

"I THOUGHT YOU WOULD BUILD THE HOUSE IN FRONT OF THE &%$#!@* WATERFALL, NOT OVER IT."

Edward J. Kaufman's remark to the architect and builder, Frank Lloyd Wright, about his weekend house built in 1939 at Mill Run, Pennsylvania. (see page 78)

The "F" Word /74

"AUGUST, WHY DON'T YOU GO OUT AND PAINT A FRUIT BASKET OR A &%$#!@* FLORAL LANDSCAPE LIKE YOUR CONTEMPORARIES?"

Madame Claude Renoir, 1905

The "F" Word /75

"CLEAN UNDERWEAR!!...MOM, IF I WAS IN AN ACCIDENT I'D PROBABLY SHIT MY &%$#!@* PANTS ANYWAY."

YOU KNOW, IF I PUT TOGETHER MY BEST &%$#!@* SCORES ON EVERY HOLE AT THE MASTERS, I'D HAVE A 48. NO SHIT."

Jack Nicholas
Besides that, the birdie on the 18th at the Old Course this year gave Jack 457 life-time birdies for The Open.

The "F" Word /76

D. Cermak Pisa 2000

"Who the &%$# is trying to drive away with the tower?"
Concerned souvenir shop owner in Pisa

"What the &%$# did that raven say again?"
Edgar Allen Poe

Angelina doesn't gave a &%$# what Brad does when he's away, as long as he doesn't have a good time."

Health nuts are going to feel stupid someday, lying in &%$#!@* hospitals dying of nothing!"

(Ponderism)

THANKS FOR THE MEMORY...

A real patriot, humanitarian, ambassador of good will and the quintessential funnyman. Ask anyone that served in the armed forces who it was that literally came right onto the &%$#!@* battlefield each year to bring good cheer to our men and women fighting overseas.

BOB Leslie Towns HOPE

"IF YOU GET CAUGHT ON A GOLF COURSE DURING A STORM AND ARE AFRAID OF LIGHTENING, HOLD UP A &%$#!@* 1-IRON. NOT EVEN GOD CAN HIT A 1-IRON."

Lee Trevino

Don Cermak, copyist, 2006

Frank Lloyd Wright
1867-1959

Regarded as one of the greatest &%$#!@* architects of the 20th century, Mr. Wright's curiosity and innovations were ahead of his time. His concept of organic architecture: the harmonious union of art and nature redefined the possibilities of architects forever.

Aside from the Guggenheim Museum in New York, probably his most famous accomplishment is Fallingwater, the house that was the week-end home of the Kaufmans from 1937 until 1963 when it was entrusted to the Western Pennsylvania Conservatory by Edward Kaufman Jr. (sic). It is the only Wright work to come into the public domain with its setting, original furnishings and art work intact. It has been listed as one of the 10 most important historical places to visit. For more information call (724) 329-8501. (See Fallingwater - page 73) www.paconserve.org

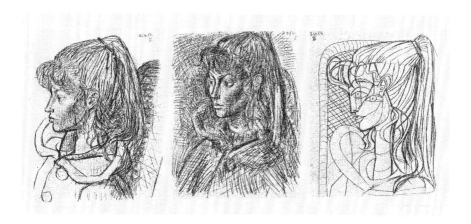

"NOW THAT LOOKS &%$#!@* MORE LIKE IT, PABLO.
YOU OUGHT TO DO MORE THINGS LIKE THIS."

Picasso's three sketches that led to the portrait
of Sylvette Davis in 1954 on page 80.

Brian Lara, West Indies cricket captain, complained that the board kept selecting batsmen who would not make the final cut. After seeing his pacer break down after the second Test match, Lara said he needed a genuine pacer. But he did not find favor with the selectors and even when he asked for a specialist spinner, which was not granted. This all happened while Lara was unaware of the fact that he had been ratified as a selector since May. "I know it's a sport, but what the &%$# are they talking about?"

An American Specator

"HAVE I GOT A &%$#!@* DEAL FOR YOU!"
Howie Mandell, Deal or No Deal

Picasso Museum, Paris

"So I put on a little &%$#!@* weight, so what? You came to hear me sing, not see me dance."

Elvis Presley

Gardening rule: When weeding, the best way to make sure you are removing a weed and not a valuable plant is to pull on it. If it comes out of the ground easily, it's a &%$#!@* valuable plant.

(A Ponderism)

The "F" Word /81

Copyist Don Cermak 2007

THE &%$#!@* BELLS HAVEN'T TOLLED NOR THE SUN RISE FOR ME IN A LONG TIME SINCE I CHECKED OUT.
Ernest Hemingway

WORLD'S EASIEST &%$#!@* QUIZ - OH YEAH!

1) How long did the hundred years war last?
2) Which country makes Panama hats?
3) From which animal do we get catgut?
4) In which month does Russia celebrate the Oct. Revolution
5) What is a camel's hair brush made of?
6) The Pacific Canary Islands are named after what animal?
7) What was King George VI's first name?
8) What color is a purple finch?
9) Where are Chinese gooseberries from?
10) How long did the Thirty Years War last?

Answers can be found on page 106. They may &%$#!@* surprise you.

"THEY NEVER SAID IT WAS &%$#!@* ICEBERG PROOF.
E.J. Smith, Captain of the Titanic

"NOW LET ME GET THIS STRAIGHT. **YOU** ARE GONNA MAKE **ME** A &%$#!@* OFFER I CAN'T REFUSE!"
Marlon Brando, The Godfather, 1972

"QUEEN ELIZABETH II LOOKED WONDERFUL WHEN SHE ATTENDED THE MILITARY TATTOO IN EDINBURGH DURING HER GOLDEN JUBILEE YEAR. I NEVER THOUGHT SHE WOULD CLIMB ALL THOSE &%$#!@* STEPS TO GET TO HER BOX, WHICH WAS JUST ABOVE US, BUT SHE DID AND PASSED WITHIN ARMS LENGTH OF ME SO I COULD TAKE THIS PICTURE, SHE EVEN STOPPED TO CHAT FOR A SECOND."

The Author at Edinburgh, Scotland, 2002

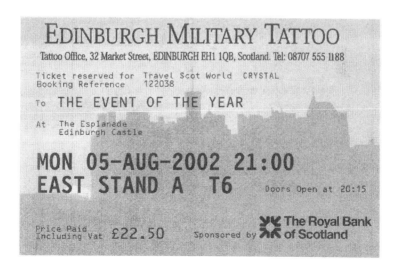

"I always said I wanted to have more &%$#!@* money than I knew what to do with."
Oprah Winfrey

"And that's the &%$#!@* way it is."
Walter Cronkite

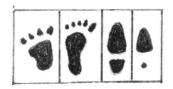

The &%$#!@* Evolution of Authority

The "F" Word /85

"AFTER NINE &%$#!@* HARD MONTHS I
END UP WITH SOMETHING LIKE THIS!"
Mia Farrow - Rosemary's Baby, 1968

"ANYONE SEE WHICH WAY THE BARBER'S TENT
BLEW DURING THAT &%$#!@* SAND STORM?"

The "F" Word /86

"Just take some of this stuff here, and add a little of that there and mix it, like such, then - BAM - kick it up a notch and you got yourself a &%$#!@* dish to die for. Besides, you'll also have the best &%$#!@* orts you could ask for. Oh yeah, Babe!"
Emeril Lagasse's The Essence of Emeril TV show

Remember, it's always the second &%$#!@* mouse that gets the cheese!

"I spent a lot of &%$#!@* money on fast cars, women and alcohol. The rest I just squandered."
Richard Pryor

"MY GET UP AND GO, GOT UP AND WENT!"
Sean Connery 007

Copyist Don Cermak

ZORBA, SELF PORTRAIT

Anthony Quinn said, "In every man, there lives a Zorba, the ultimate free soul daring to celebrate victory and to dismiss defeat. He moves to the frenzied beat of the music, our world whirls and we are transformed into the soul of Zorba."

"Mr. Quinn was a true renaissance man who captured the passion of his world acclaimed role of Zorba in his art work.

"We were invited to come to New York in 1989 for a weekend trip at the Trump Plaza to see his Art Exhibition and preview his new sculpture, paintings and drawings before they were made available to the general public. Many of his friends, including Tom Selleck, Charlton Heston, and Ricardo Mautalabam, turned out to pay homage to this great actor and newly acclaimed artist, including President Ronald Reagan who accepted sculptures for The Presidential Collection. It was a spectacular weekend for all."

The Author

The "F" Word /88

"You can take this &%$#!@* job and shove it."
Lyndon B. Johnson, 1968

"This is my &%$#!@* pet pussy, boys.
Would you like to pet her?"
African Safari Guide

The "F" Word / 89

"I'M NEW AT THIS BUT I KNOW I CAN GET US OUT OF HERE ONCE I FIGURE OUT WHERE THE &%$# WE ARE."
Amsterdam water taxi

HEY, FRED. THERE'S A &%$#!@* GUY OVER HERE WHO SMELLS LIKE HE COULD BE YOUR BROTHER.

The "F" Word /90

Janzten, Inc

"It's the latest &%$#!@* Olympic fashion."
Johnny Weismuller 1924 Olympics

"Never have so &%$#!@* few eaten so &%$#!@* much in so short a &%$#!@* time!"

Head Chef on the QE2 paraphrasing Winston Churchill on baked Alaska night

The "F" Word /91

"YOU GO THAT WAY AND I'LL GO THIS WAY
AND WE'LL SURPRISE THE DUMB &%$#."
Velocirapters, Jurassic Park, 1993

"I COULD HAVE BEEN SOME &%$#!@* BODY
INSTEAD OF A BUM, WHICH IS WHAT I AM. IT WAS
YOU, CHARLEY. I WAS YOUR BROTHER AND YOU
SHOULDA &%$#!@* LOOKED OUT FOR ME."
Marlon Brando, On The Waterfront, 1954

"You'd cry too if you sang some of the songs they ask me to sing. My &%$#!@* throat is killing me."

Janis Joplin - Woodstock, 1969

"After I tried this damn stuff none of my girlfriends would kiss me any more so I'm going back to smoking &%$#!@* butts."

Spurned Casanova

The "F" Word / 93

Bereau of Printing and Engraving

"I PERSONALLY DON'T GIVE A &%$# IF THERE'S NOT ENOUGH ROOM FOR ANYONE ELSE ON MT. RUSHMORE, ABE, WHAT ABOUT YOU?"
Andrew Jackson

"WE CALL THIS &%$#!@* GOLF LEAGUE THE SENIOR "P".G.A."

Dr. Carnivore
Psychiatrist

The author's pencil drawing

"I DUNNO, DOC. EITHER I'M GETTING OLD OR THE &%$#!@* ANIMALS ARE GETTING FASTER EACH YEAR DURING MIGRATION."

Anonymous

IS THIS &%$#!@* POSSIBLE?

Copyist Don Cermak

Leonardo da Vinci was 30 when he wrote to the Duke of Milan recommending himself "with the utmost humility" as an architect. engineer, inventor, expert on irrigation, a designer of military equipment and strategist of sieges. He climaxed this catalogue of his talents with these words: "I can carry out sculpture in marble, bronze and clay, and also can do painting whatever may be done as well as any other, be he who he may."

"What a &%$#!@* understatement. 'The Madonna of the Rocks' was painted between 1483-1490 - 20 years before the Mona Lisa. I picked out one of the four figures in this large painting (15'-9" X 10'-3"), the angel Uriel and did this painting in oil. The model for Uriel was said to be Cecilia Gallerini, the Duke's mistress who also posed for Leonardo's 'Lady with an Ermine'.."

The Author

"Why didn't you tell me not to take the &%$#!@* stairs?"

The "F" Word / 97

"Forget that &%$#!@* Boogie Woogie Sam.
You know what I want to hear. You played
it for her and you can play it for me."
Humphrey Bogart, Casablanca

"What the &%$# do you mean these
rides are only for kids?"
Walt Disney

ACROSS THE THRESHOLD

"I don't know if this &%$#!@* thing will ever amount to much, Orville, it's too heavy."
Wilber Wright, 1902

D. Cermak St. Petersburg

"How long do you think it would &%$#!@* take you to see all the art in the Hermitage if you spent only one minute looking at all the collections?

"The Winter Palace where Catherine the Great began her collections, in a special part of the palace set aside for unofficial receptions, was called by the French name, Hermitage, suggesting a place of solitude. It contains over 2,800,000 works of art. It would take a person viewing 24 hrs a day, seven days a week, 52 weeks a year more than 24 &%$#!@* Years. Believe it or not. And once you are there try to find a &%$#!@* toilet when you need one. If you do get to St. Petersburg, Russia, though, it's worth a visit, or two.

The Author

"The first time I played the Masters, I was so &%$#!@* nervous I drank a bottle of rum before I teed off and shot the happiest 83 of my life."

Chi Chi Rodriguez

"TO THE PERSON WHO YELLED OUT THAT I NEED SOME GUITAR LESSONS, I SAY, ARE YOU &%$#!@* KIDDING?"
Jerry Garcia of The Grateful Dead - 1942-1995

"Winning isn't everything. It's the only &%$#!@* thing."
Vince Lombardi

"If assholes were pilots Congress would be one, big &%$#!@* airport."

"I don't know why the &%$# I'm here. I didn't do anything!"
Saddam Hussein

The deposed dictator, who insisted on being addressed as The President of Iraq, during his trial, has told his jailers next to nothing, and interrogated the judge demanding to know under what authority he was holding the hearing.

The "F" Word /102

"Hey boy! Is looking for &%$#!@* needles all you can think about?"
Dollyland Parton

"Here's to all those people who don't drink 'cause when they wake up in the morning that's as &%$#!@* good as they're gonna feel all day."
Dean Martin

"Joe said, all I want is a little &%$#!@* more than I'll ever get" "Joe who?"
Jo Mama

"Do you think the kingdom will fall today, Derrick?" "Only if the &%$#!@* birds leave! God save the Ravens."

Derrick Coyle, Tower of London's Raven Master with two Beefeaters that stand guard.

Legend has it that if these birds, who have roamed the courtyard of England's Tower of London for centuries, ever leave the tower, the fortress and the Kingdom will fall. The current flock have now - like Anne Boleyn and Sir Walter Raleigh - been imprisoned within its walls. Concerned that the birds might succumb to avian Flu, the Raven Master built cages inside the 11th century stronghold and moved the Birds into them in 2004.

Helen Starkweather

The "F" Word /104

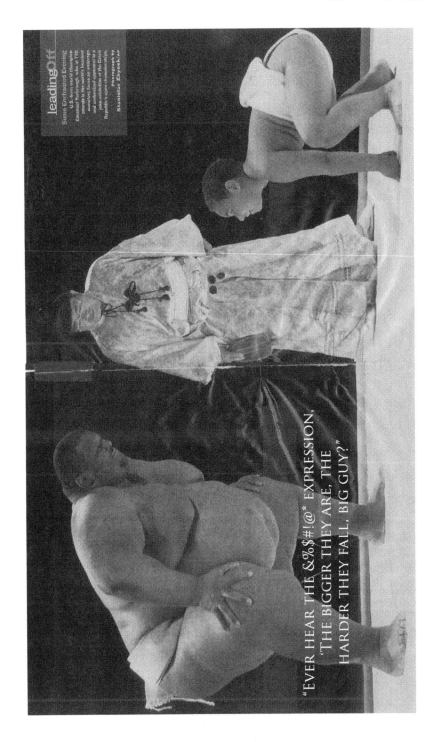

Copyist Don Cermak 1996

VINCENT VAN GOGH
1853 - 1890

"This artist, whose paintings are worth millions, sold only one &%$#!@* painting during his lifetime for a measly 400 francs. Oddly enough he painted 37 self portraits and committed suicide at the age of 37. No wonder the despiration in his eyes in all his portraits looked like he was reaching into his soul.

Answers for page 15

Longest Palindrome - A Man, A Plan, A Canal, Panama

Hazardous

abstemious & facetious

Answer to world's easiest quiz
1) 116 years
2) Ecuador
3) Sheep & horses
4) November
5) Squirrel fur
6) Dogs
7) Albert
8) Crimson
9) New Zealand
10) 30 years

Now relax and concentrate on the 4 small dots in the middle of the picture for about 40 seconds, then take a look at a wall (any smooth single colored surface). Start blinking and you will see my inspiration for this book.

About The Author

After college, Mr. Cermak, who had aspirations of becoming an artist or professional athlete, saw there were too many starving artists around. He also discovered there were more men devoted to golf who were just eking out a living while giving the game their full time and attention. This was more than he was able to give so he went to work for his father who was a pioneer in the plastic tile industry. He soon discovered that this was not exactly his cup of tea either so he went to an executive search firm to see what they could do for him. The firm offered him a job in their administrative department which he took, his thinking being that if the right job came along he would take it and pay the placement fee himself.

He enjoyed the work so much that he left after 6 months to form his own agency and specialized in educational placement to overseas schools.

The business afforded him the time to become a professional bowler and charter member of the PBA. It also allowed him to spend time with Harry Reese, head pro at the Ridgewood Country Club, to improve and learn more about the game. This proved beneficial because it enabled him to become a golf instructor for several cruise lines after he retired.

It was during this time that he wrote and illustrated an instructional book on golf titled, 'Be A Swinger'. After this he started writing a novel and was part way through it when he got the idea for the "F" word book after reading 'On Bullshit' by Harry G. Frankfurt.

He still paints on a commission basis and is currently in what he refers to as his 'pastel period' painting masterpieces in pastel rather than oil, which he feels is more challenging. He considers himself a good copyist and features several of his paintings in this book.

Made in the USA
Columbia, SC
07 December 2022